PROTECTING OUR PLANET

By Jilly Hunt

EADLINES BEYOND THE HEADLINES BEYOND THE HEAD

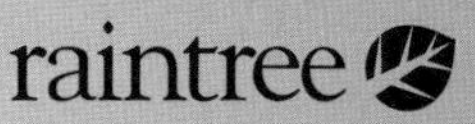
raintree
a Capstone company — publishers for children

Raintree is an imprint of Capstone Global Library Limited, a company incorporated in England and Wales having its registered office at 7 Pilgrim Street, London, EC4V 6LB – Registered company number: 6695582

www.raintreepublishers.co.uk
myorders@raintreepublishers.co.uk

First published in hardback in 2017

Edited by Adrian Vigliano
Designed by Philippa Jenkins
Original illustrations © Capstone Global Library Limited 2017
Illustrated by Oxford Designers and Illustrators
Picture research by Morgan Walters
Production by Tori Abraham
Originated by Capstone Global Library Ltd
Printed and bound in China

ISBN 978 1 4747 4920 6
21 20 19 18 17
10 9 8 7 6 5 4 3 2 1

British Library Cataloguing in Publication Data
A full catalogue record for this book is available from the British Library.

Acknowledgements
We would like to thank the following for permission to reproduce photographs: Alamy: Art Directors & TRIP, 23, Ashley Cooper pics, 19; Capstone Press: Philippa Jenkins, map 1, 34, 36, ipad 8, 13, 23, 29, 31, 41; Getty Images: Cameron Davidson, 27, EZEQUIEL BECERRA, 22; iStockphoto: upheaval, 1; NASA/JPL, 13; Newscom: A3250 Oliver Berg Deutsch Presse Agentur, 35, FRANCIS R. MALASIG/EPA, 28, Pacific Press/Sipa USA, 31; Science Source: Jessica Wilson/ NASA, spread 16-17; Shutterstock: 46design, 41, AlessandraRC, 37, AustralianCamera, 32, canghai76, 42, Catalin Petolea, 14, Dewi Putra, 15, Evan El-Amin, top inset 12, f11photo, 8, Frederic Legrand - COMEO, bottom inset 12, Geet Theerawat, 43, Guliyev, Cover (turbine), Jess Wealleans, 9, Jorge Salcedo, Cover (leaves) design element throughout, Leonard Zhukovsky, 25, manfredxy, 6, Marie Dirgova, 38, Michael Zysman, 10, MO_SES Premium, 4, Petr Kovalenkov, (eiffle) 12, Rich Carey, 29, 33, Sakurra, 7, Sean Locke Photography, 40, Smit, 11, Spaceport9, 21, ssguy, 20, Taina Sohlman, 24, Tigergallery, 26, Tonkinphotography, spread 4-5, vwPix, 30

We would like to thank Michelle Fournier, Interpretive Naturalist, Chippewa Nature Center, Midland, MI, USA, for her invaluable help in the preparation of this book.

CONTENTS

Some words are shown in bold, **like this**. You can find out what they mean by looking in the glossary.

Chapter 1

WHAT'S BEYOND THE HEADLINES ABOUT OUR ENVIRONMENT?

"EXTREME WEATHER CAUSED BY GLOBAL WARMING"

"HUMANKIND UNABLE TO STOP RISING TEMPERATURES"

"ENVIRONMENTAL POLLUTION HITS RECORD HIGH"

We've all seen headlines like this about our environment. But how much do we really know about these issues?

The environment is the world around us. We often use the word to describe the natural world or our physical surroundings, especially when it is being affected by human activity. Environmental issues make the news because many people are concerned about the damage that human activity is doing. Scientists warn that some human activity, such as the burning of fossil fuels, is causing irreversible changes which will affect environments around the world forever.

DID YOU KNOW?

Aluminium is the most recyclable of all materials. Recycling just one aluminium can saves enough energy to power a TV for three hours.

Who cares?

Different groups of people around the world are interested in environmental issues for different reasons. Governments are mostly interested in the environment in terms of the economic benefits that it can bring to their country. An example would be how a given nation might make money from selling its natural resources such as coal or oil. Governments must also consider the needs and wants of their people, and the money they have available. For example, they must consider the need for more houses if the country's population is growing. Governments may have agencies that are dedicated to protecting a particular area of the environment, such as national parks or key wildlife areas.

The United Nations (UN) is a group of countries that try to work together to agree on rules to protect the world. They have an agency that focuses on the environment.

Non-Government Organizations (NGOs), such as Greenpeace or World Wide Fund for Nature, are concerned with how humans interact with the natural environment and the impact this has on the environment. They often **lobby** governments to try to influence government decisions in favour of protecting the environment.

DID YOU KNOW?

The first UN conference about the environment was held in 1972. Issues that were discussed included protecting whales, chemical pollution and atomic bomb testing.

A brief history of environmental issues

We hear on the news about rising sea levels and **climate change** and how human activity has caused it. How did this happen?

Human activity began to have a significant effect on the environment over 200 years ago with the start of the **Industrial Revolution** in England, which then spread to Europe and North America. The Industrial Revolution marked a change from a mainly agricultural way of life to a more industrial one. It began when fabric and clothing industries introduced the latest technological innovations, such as looms, to speed up the manufacturing process. Many of these innovations required power, which was often provided by steam engines fuelled by coal.

▲ The spread of industry through the world brought with it an increase in greenhouse gases and environmental pollution.

We know now that burning fossil fuels, such as coal, gas or oil, causes pollution and releases harmful carbon dioxide (CO_2) into the air. But at the time of the Industrial Revolution, there was a lack of knowledge about environmental impact. The advantages of industrialization seemed to be so great that no one was worried about what was happening to nature.

The greenhouse effect

The greenhouse effect is the way Earth stays warm. Energy from the Sun is trapped by gases in Earth's **atmosphere**. Greenhouse gases stop this heat from escaping, which keeps Earth warm. The gases that trap the energy include methane and carbon dioxide. Scientists believe that human activity is increasing the amount of these greenhouse gases. The gases are then trapping more of the Sun's energy and causing our planet to heat up. A warming climate has many negative effects on the planet. Polar regions are especially vulnerable, as warmer temperatures can lead to melting glaciers and rising ocean levels around the world.

The greenhouse effect

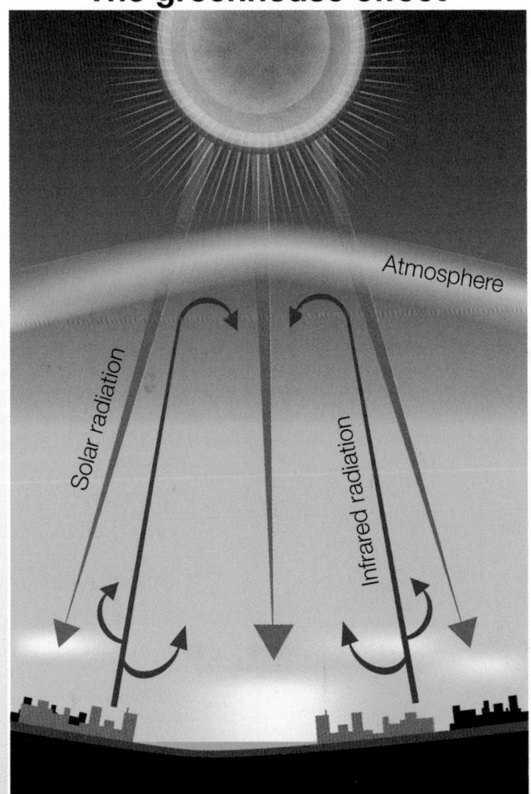

Greenhouse gases absorb heat energy from the Sun, resulting in global warming.

DID YOU KNOW?

We need the greenhouse effect to keep Earth warm. Without it the average temperature would be –18°C (0°F).

The increase in human population has led to increased pollution.

A growing population

Industrialization has been accompanied by an increase in the world's population. More people means more food is needed for them to eat, and more space is needed for them to live in. Providing this has caused environmental problems such as **deforestation** and pollution.

People have taken a more industrial approach to growing food, which has not always been good for the environment. For example, in the past, farmers used plants such as chrysanthemums or tobacco, which were toxic to insects or rodents but didn't harm the environment. However, after **World War II**, scientists had developed a way of making **chemical pesticides** to stop crops from being eaten by pests. What people didn't yet realize was that these chemical pesticides were also killing other animals, especially birds and fish.

THINK ABOUT IT

Zhang lives in the Chinese city of Beijing and is a tennis coach. He can afford to buy meat but his life wasn't always so comfortable. As a child of rural farmers, he often went hungry.

Zhang eats meat every day now, but the global demand for meat is putting pressure on our environment. Should the amount of meat people can eat be restricted? Should everyone be allowed the same amount of food no matter where they live?

Intensive farming

Animal farming also became more industrialized and intensive to try to produce more food, more cheaply and more quickly. In this kind of farming, livestock animals such as cows, pigs, sheep and chickens are confined to small spaces in conditions that are not natural for them. Intensive livestock farming can cause pollution if animal waste contaminates water supplies. People also have concerns about the welfare of the animals.

DID YOU KNOW?

The world's livestock are responsible for 18 per cent of global greenhouse gas emissions.

Rearing cattle uses more water and creates more pollution than growing crops.

Changing lifestyles

As lifestyles have changed, the demand for more processed, 'fast' foods such as beef burgers has increased. Farming cattle takes more water than growing crops and cattle require more land on which to graze. Trees are cut down to make space to keep more cattle, which has a double impact on the environment. The trees that absorb harmful carbon dioxide are removed and replaced with animals that add to greenhouse gases.

Chapter 2

WHAT'S BEYOND THE HEADLINES ABOUT GLOBAL WARMING?

Global warming is making headlines because it is so important and links in with many other environmental issues. For example, increases in extreme weather conditions are linked to climate change, which is driven by our increasingly industrial lifestyles. Around the world we burn fossil fuels to heat or cool our homes, power our industries and fuel our vehicles. All this human activity increases the amount of greenhouse gases in our environment. This drives up the temperature of our planet, which causes weather extremes *and* can cause water, air and land pollution.

Awareness of the greenhouse effect

Scientists have actually been aware of the "greenhouse effect" for hundreds of years, although they might not have fully understood the consequences of it. In 1824, the French scientist Joseph Fourier was the first person to show that an increase in carbon dioxide in Earth's atmosphere would lead to global warming.

Changes to Earth's climate cause ice in polar regions to melt.

Why do we need to worry about global warming?

One of the concerns about global warming is the melting of land ice because it causes sea levels to rise. Land ice is found in mountain glaciers and the ice sheets covering Greenland and Antarctica. Sea ice is also melting, but since it's already in the sea it doesn't cause sea levels to rise. However, melting sea ice does add to global warming. Sea ice reflects the sun's rays but the deep, dark ocean absorbs the sun's rays and warms up, which causes more land ice to melt.

Weather worries

Another important effect of climate change is the impact it will have on the world's weather. Scientists predict that as the world's temperature increases we will see more severe storms and changes in **precipitation**, which could mean floods in some areas and droughts in others.

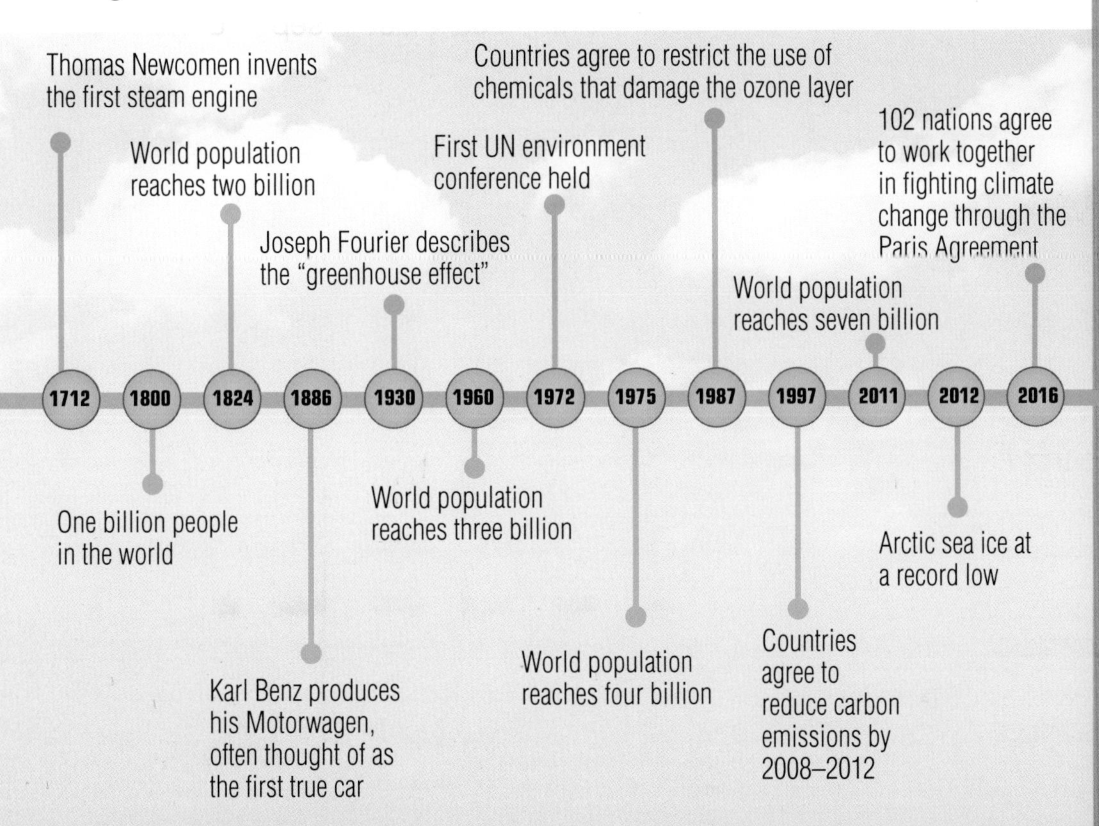

What is being done to reduce climate change?

The good news about climate change is that nations are coming together to try to reduce their **emissions** of greenhouse gases and combat rising temperatures. In October 2016, 102 nations agreed to the UN Framework Convention on Climate Change, also known as the Paris Agreement. For the first time, all these nations have committed to tackle this massive global problem. China and the US, the world's two largest emitters, signed the agreement in 2016.

The aims of the Paris Agreement

The main aim of the Paris Agreement is to keep the rise in the world's temperature to under 2°C (36°F) by the end of the 21st century, preferably limiting the rise to only 1.5°C (35°F).

Rank	Nation	CO_2 emissions total (in thousand metric tons of carbon)
1	China (mainland)	2,795,054
2	United States of America	1,414,281
3	India	554,882
4	Russian Federation	487,885
5	Japan	339,074

This table shows the top five most polluting countries in terms of CO_2 emissions in 2013.

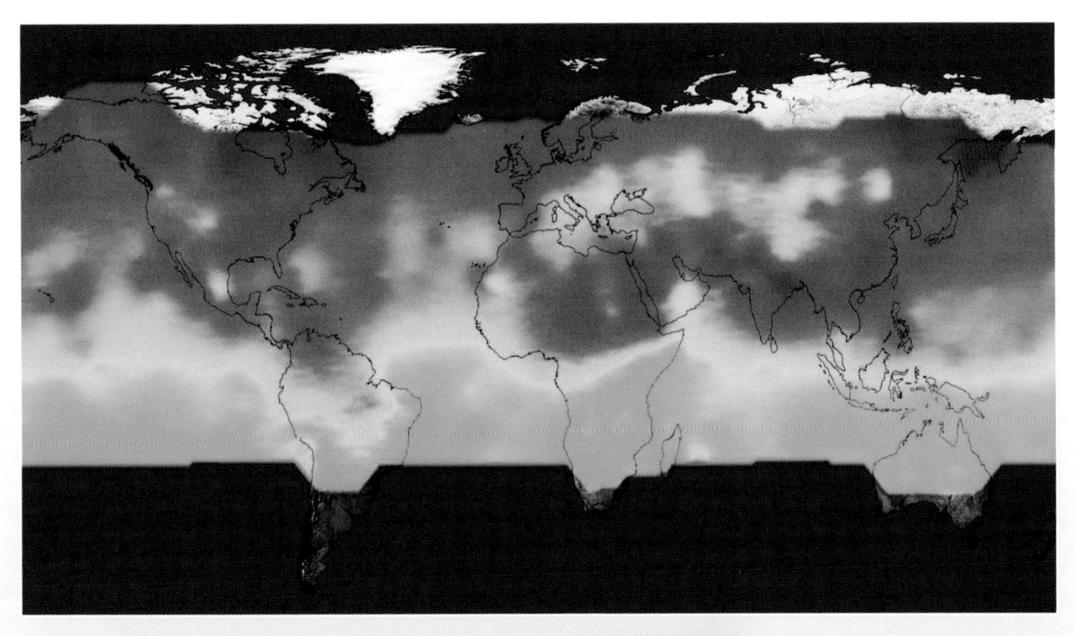

NASA has developed tools for producing images such as this. These images help scientists study global carbon dioxide levels.

THINK ABOUT IT

The Paris Agreement bans any country from leaving the agreement for three years and then they must give a year-long notice period. Why do you think this is part of the deal?

How are countries planning to reduce carbon emissions?

Before the Paris Agreement came into effect, each nation put forward plans about how they intended to cut emissions and move to more **renewable energy** supplies. Renewable energy supplies pollute less than non-renewables such as coal. The nations then had a meeting to make these plans more detailed.

They have a variety of plans to try to reduce **carbon** emissions. For example, Canada is introducing a carbon tax. Other countries are introducing a carbon pricing system like the one China already has in place.

Carbon pricing and carbon tax

A carbon pricing system works by giving industries an allowance for a total level of greenhouse gas emissions. Those industries with low emissions can sell their extra allowances to industries that need larger emission allowances.

A carbon tax is a price set on greenhouse gas emissions. The more gas a company emits, the more tax it has to pay. The more tax a company pays, the less profit it makes. So, companies are going to want to try to reduce greenhouse gas emissions.

GOOD NEWS

In October 2016, the first deal to limit greenhouse gas emissions from aeroplanes was agreed by the International Civil Aviation Organization (ICAO). From 2020 onwards any increase in emissions will need to be offset by actions such as planting trees.

DID YOU KNOW?

2016 was the warmest year since records began. 2017 has continued the trend of record-setting highs in average temperature around the world.

People in developing countries tend to be the most vulnerable to climate change impacts such as flooding.

How countries are helping each other

The effects of climate change have been felt the hardest by people in developing countries, such as Sub-Saharan Africa and South Asia. They have experienced severe droughts or flooding. Some countries, like the island nation of Kiribati, could disappear forever if sea levels continue to rise. Yet it is the richer countries who are responsible for the higher emissions of greenhouse gases. As part of the Paris Agreement, richer countries have committed billions of dollars to help poorer countries adapt to climate change. However, discussions are still taking place as to whether richer countries should pay for the damage in poorer countries caused by climate change.

The ozone hole

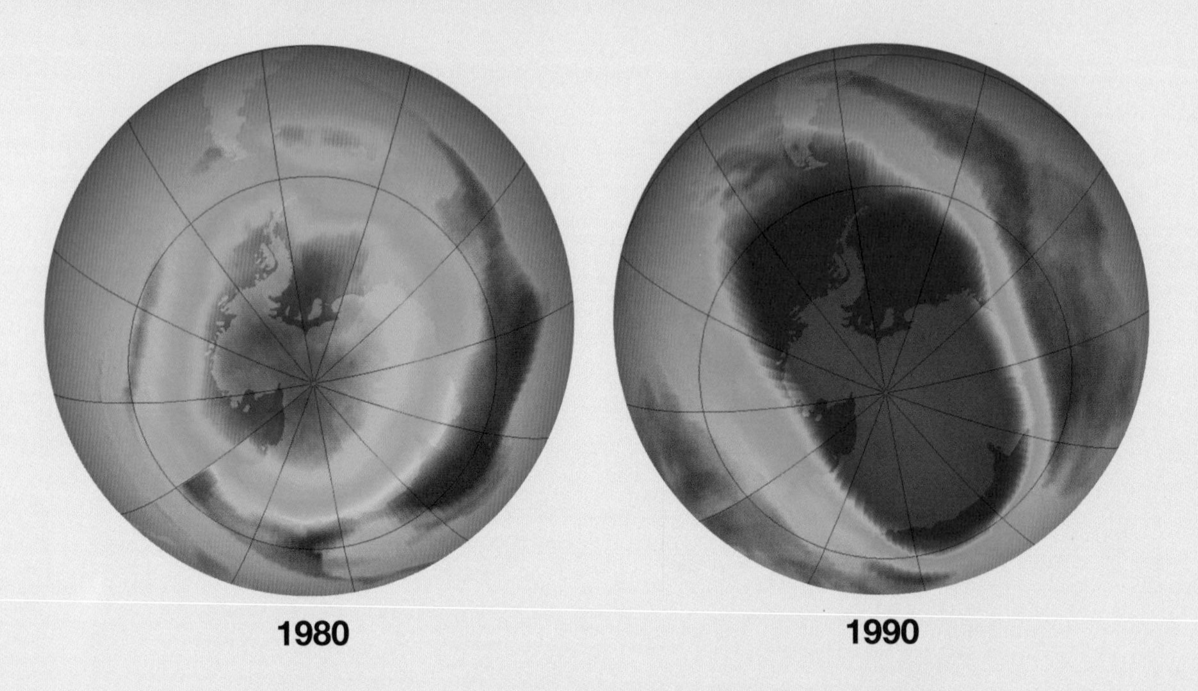

1980 1990

Ozone is a gas that occurs naturally in the stratosphere, which is the middle layer of Earth's atmosphere. Ozone has an important job to do because it blocks out harmful **ultraviolet** (UV) rays from the Sun that would otherwise damage plants and animals. Too much exposure to UV rays can injure eyes and cause sunburn and skin cancer.

In the 1980s, scientists made the worrying discovery of a thinning or a "hole" in the ozone layer, which was particularly bad over Antarctica. Some people didn't believe that human activity was affecting the planet. But now scientists were able to show that the thinning of the ozone layer had a clear link with the gases that were being used in our everyday lives.

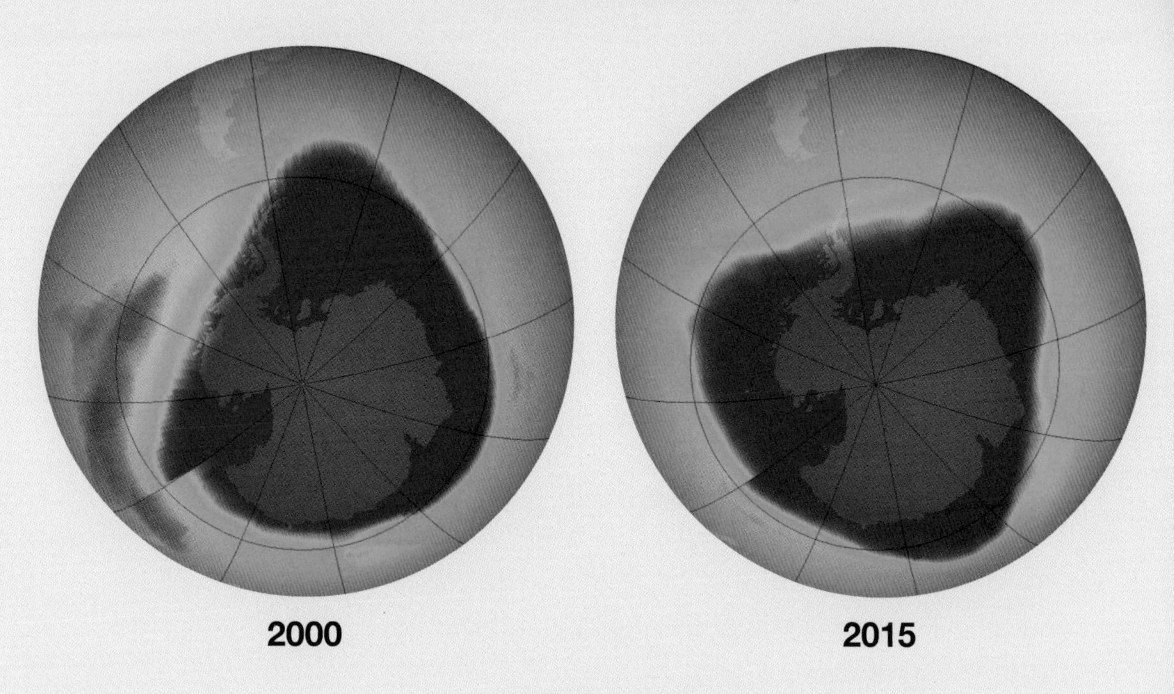

▼ The efforts at reducing the hole in the ozone layer seem to be working.

How did the hole happen?

The thinning of the ozone layer has happened because of an increase in chemicals in the atmosphere that break down ozone. Scientists discovered that these chemicals, called chlorofluorocarbons and hydrochlorofluorocarbons, or CFCs and HFCs for short, were regularly used around the world in aerosols, refrigerators and air conditioning units.

Taking action

The world took notice of this scientific evidence and in 1987 the UN put in place a global agreement called the Montreal Protocol. The aim of this agreement is to phase out the use of the chemicals that are causing damage to the ozone layer.

In 2003, then-Secretary General of the UN, Kofi Annan, said that the Montreal Protocol has been “the single most successful international agreement to date”. Scientists have been able to show that the ozone layer is slowly starting to regenerate.

Chapter 3

WHAT'S BEYOND THE HEADLINES ABOUT CLEANER ENERGY?

Science shows us the damage that burning fossil fuels is doing to our environment. In addition, it also shows how fossil fuels contribute to global warming. We also know that fossil fuels are a limited resource, although when exactly they will run out is an area of disagreement amongst the experts. What we do know is that it is important for us to find alternative, cleaner, renewable energy sources.

What are cleaner energy sources?

The good news is that the natural world actually provides a plentiful supply of cleaner, renewable energy, if we can find ways to harness it. Different countries have more of some renewable energy sources than others.

This table shows a range of cleaner, renewable energy sources that will help us reduce carbon emissions.

Energy source	How energy is harnessed
Solar	Energy from the Sun's rays is captured by panels and converted into electricity. The positioning of the panels is important so as not to harm wildlife or damage trees or plants.
Wind	Wind is used to drive **turbines** to generate electricity. The location of wind turbines is important. If they are placed in migration corridors millions of migrating birds may be killed.
Tidal	The movement of the tides drive turbines, which can be used to generate electricity.
Hydroelectric	The movement of water through a turbine. Usually water is stored using a dam and a reservoir. A big flow of water is then released from a great height to turn the turbines and generate electricity. Large hydroelectric power schemes do have negative environmental impacts.
Bioenergy	Energy gained from plant materials, such as the ethanol that is naturally made when yeasts feed on sugar. The way the plants are grown can have an impact on the environment. For example the use of pesticides or the clearing of land in order to grow crops.
Geothermal	Energy from within the ground is converted into electricity.

DID YOU KNOW?

Tidal power is actually not a new innovation — the ancient Egyptians also used this method to power mills to grind grain.

Wave energy generators, such as this one in Scotland, are one way of harnessing hydroelectric power. ▼

Increased investment in renewable energy

Converting to cleaner, renewable energy does involve spending money. Harnessing the energy requires different equipment from that which is used to convert fossil fuels into power. Many countries also want to do more research to find newer technology that may be even more efficient. In 2015, six times more was invested globally into renewable energy than ever before. The fact that less was invested into gas or coal-fired sources of electricity than into renewable energy is also another big step forward.

GOOD NEWS

China is one of the world's largest emitters of greenhouse gases, so it is good news that they are also one of the world's biggest investors in renewable energy. In 2015, they invested £84 billion ($103 billion) in renewable energy, which is 36 per cent of the world's total investment.

China has made a significant commitment to solar and wind power, often both at the same time.

Leading the way

Developing countries are now investing more into renewable energy than developed countries are. In 2015, they invested a total of £127 billion ($156 billion) into renewables.

GOOD NEWS

Small businesses and community groups are taking advantage of cheaper costs and introducing solar energy across Africa. Portable solar kiosks have been introduced in Tanzania and Rwanda to allow access to electricity for small businesses. Specially adapted shipping containers have been used in South Africa and Mali to protect the valuable solar panels from theft. It is hoped access to cheap electricity will improve lives and provide new job opportunities for those most in need. For example, before people in Mali had electricity they were forced to throw away any excess goat's milk because they couldn't keep it cool and fresh. But now they can use their electricity to make cheese to sell.

Portable solar energy panels can be especially useful to people in the developing world.

Solar energy provides opportunities for countries, such as those in Sub-Saharan Africa, that do not already have an established supply of electricity. And sunshine is a resource they have in abundance. The cost to set up solar panels has decreased, which makes this method of electricity generation more accessible.

Costa Rica

The Central American country of Costa Rica made global headlines in 2015 after it used only renewable energy for 75 days. The country managed this thanks to their four hydroelectric plants and some heavy rainfall. The country's other sources of renewable energy are the many volcanoes that provide geothermal energy. Geothermal energy comes from Earth's natural heat sources.

Committed to renewable energy

Costa Rica's government is committed to renewable energy. The country aims to be carbon-neutral by 2021 by balancing carbon released into the atmosphere with sustainable efforts. Costa Rica does not want to rely on fossil fuels, so have invested in new geothermal projects. Although hydropower supplied 80 per cent of their energy in 2014, they know that a period of drought could threaten their country's energy supply.

Geothermal power is one important renewable energy resource for Costa Rica. ▲

DID YOU KNOW?

Hydroelectric power is the largest renewable source of electricity and currently provides about 20 per cent of the world's energy.

THINK ABOUT IT

Around the world, nearly 500 million people have been harmed by the use of hydropower. When dams are being built, they may need to take over people's farmland and homes, forcing them to move. Dams can affect people's water supply as rivers are diverted, as well as damage the environment and harm animals. Experts think that smaller plans have more potential and are more environmentally friendly. What do you think? Should dams be built regardless of the damage they may do in order to provide drinking water, prevent floods and produce power?

Cleaner energy on our streets

Transport emissions make up about 14 per cent of the world's greenhouse gas emissions. There are a number of ways that these emissions could be reduced:

- Switching to electricity generated by renewable sources.
- Improving technology to make vehicles use less fuel.
- Reducing fuel demand by providing, for example, cycle paths or public transport powered by cleaner energy.

This pie chart shows global greenhouse gas emissions in 2010.

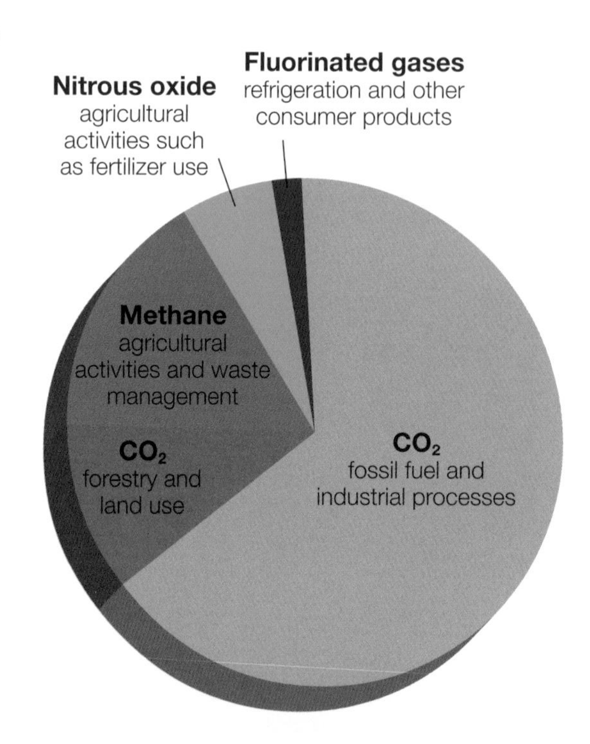

Most forms of transport rely on burning fossil fuels in the form of petrol and diesel.

Greener trucking

One way that is being tested to reduce emissions from long-distance lorry journeys is "platooning". This is where lorries travel in convoy, connected by wireless technology. Each lorry has a driver but it is only the vehicle at the front that actually drives. This lead truck controls the lorries behind it, which allows them to all travel at a consistent, safe speed. Experts say that platooning can lead to a 15 per cent saving in fuel, and therefore fewer emissions.

Sharing

In cities around the world there are car-sharing schemes. Members usually pay a yearly fee to have access to a car when they need it. They then pay an hourly rate when they actually use the car. Some experts estimate that sharing just one car takes another 20 off the road. This reduces traffic congestion and emissions.

Many cities also have bike schemes where users can hire a bike in the street and leave it at another sharing point in the city.

Bike sharing has become common in cities around the world.

GOOD NEWS

The parcel delivery company, UPS, is piloting electrically assisted cycles to reduce emissions on shorter journeys.

DID YOU KNOW?

Experts predict that the number of cars owned worldwide could triple to over two billion by 2050.

Chapter 4

WHAT'S BEYOND THE HEADLINES ABOUT PROTECTING OUR OCEANS?

The world's oceans are a precious resource. They contain 97 per cent of all the water on the surface of Earth. In addition to all the seafood that they provide, they also generate half the amount of oxygen that we each breathe. And yet the ocean has been neglected, used as a rubbish bin, and polluted by sewage and oil spills.

Changing seas

The human activity that has led to climate change also affects the seas and oceans. As air temperatures increase, so do ocean temperatures. This isn't good news for the many sea creatures that can only live in colder waters.

Oil spills can cause enormous harm to ocean life.

It may be surprising to learn that carbon dioxide emissions also affect our seas and oceans. Oceans absorb 30 per cent of the carbon dioxide in the atmosphere. The more carbon dioxide there is in the atmosphere, the more the oceans absorb. The increase in carbon dioxide in seawater is changing its chemical makeup and making it more acidic. This is having a big impact on corals and sea creatures with shells, such as oysters, clams and sea urchins. These creatures are finding it harder to get the chemicals they need from the seawater to build their protective shells and skeletons.

DID YOU KNOW?

Many of the things that are polluting our oceans, such as the chemicals in pesticides and fertilizers, did not exist 60 years ago.

The biggest source of pollution

The biggest source of pollution to the world's seas and oceans is actually from the land. Pollution sources can range from the large scale of agricultural fertilisers and pesticides to the smallest drops of car engine oil left by millions of vehicles every day. Rainwater washes the pollution into rivers or waterways and eventually it all ends up in the sea.

Plastic waste

The Great Pacific Garbage Patch has made headlines for being a vast area of ocean that is full of tiny bits of plastic. The water in this area is like a thick soup with some plastic items floating in it. It is growing so much that it is starting to become visible from space.

Experts estimate that in 2015, about 8 million tonnes of plastic ended up in the world's oceans. That's the same weight as about 70,000 blue whales! As well as being ugly, this plastic enters the food chain, causing illness and other problems in animal populations.

Environmental groups often lead the way in cleaning up plastic waste.

GOOD NEWS

In 2015, shops in England began charging for plastic bags. After just six months, there was an 83 per cent reduction in the use of plastic bags.

Properties of plastic

To really understand the plastic problem it helps to know about the properties of plastic. If plastic is exposed to sunlight and high temperatures, it starts to break down into smaller pieces. This happens quickly in the heat of a summer's day on land. It happens more slowly in the cold depths of an ocean where sunlight does not reach. However breaking up into smaller pieces isn't a good thing either. Small bits of plastic can be eaten by fish and other sea creatures, which are then eaten by humans. It is thought a plate of just six oysters could contain up to 50 particles of plastic.

Every year, plastic bags and other plastic waste kill an estimated 1,000,000 sea creatures.

THINK ABOUT IT

Why do we not want these tiny microplastics in the food chain? What do you think the problems might be? Try to find out more.

Microbeads

Microplastics are tiny pieces of plastic. They come from large pieces of plastic but also from synthetic fibres used to make some clothing, and from microbeads that are used in cosmetics. The problem with microplastics is their small size. It is very hard to remove them from the water or stop them entering the water in the first place.

Banning microbeads

The good news is that people are taking action. Large cosmetic companies have agreed to stop using microbeads. The US and Canada have already banned their use, and the UK have announced plans to ban the use of microbeads in cosmetics and cleaning products by 2018. The European Union are also developing proposals to ban their use.

DID YOU KNOW?

Just one shower, using scrubs and shower gels with microbeads in, could lead to 100,000 plastic particles getting into our seas and oceans.

▲ An environmental group in the Philippines works to clean up plastic waste in a bird sanctuary in 2014.

A great big clean up

Keeping beaches and waterways free from plastic litter can help the microplastics problem from getting worse.

The charity Ocean Cleanup is investigating techniques to try to remove as much plastic from the sea as possible using enormous barriers to capture debris. However, other experts think that these barriers will disturb some sea creatures, and that it would be better to focus on cleaning up the coasts of China and Indonesia where much of the plastic comes from.

THINK ABOUT IT

What next? There are millions of tonnes of plastic waste. What else could be done to reduce the use of plastic?

Chapter 5

WHAT'S BEYOND THE HEADLINES ABOUT DEFORESTATION?

Deforestation, or forest clearance, is when trees are permanently cleared from forests and woodlands. No trees are replanted. People clear forests for a number of reasons. They may want the wood to sell or use as firewood, or want the land to grow crops or graze cattle.

Forest clearance can cause many problems. The forest's wildlife are killed or left homeless. Soil erosion can mean that the rich topsoil is washed away by heavy rains or floods because there are no longer tree roots to bind it together. This is not good news for farmers because the top soil is what their crops will grow best in. They may end up using more fertilizer to counteract this, which can increase environmental pollution. Soil erosion is not good for river life because this soil ends up in rivers and waterways, clogging them up and harming wildlife.

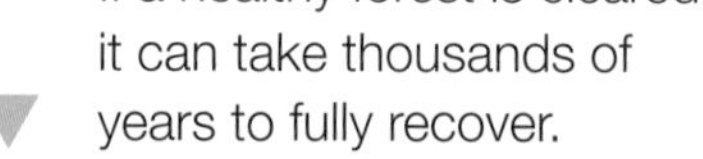
If a healthy forest is cleared, it can take thousands of years to fully recover.

Increasing carbon emissions

Deforestation is the second biggest contributor of carbon emissions. Trees are important in fighting climate change because during the process of **photosynthesis** they take in carbon dioxide and release oxygen. All deforestation is a concern, but it is especially so in the **tropics**. When tropical forests are cut down, carbon dioxide is released from the soil and adds to carbon emissions.

DID YOU KNOW?

Approximately 13 million hectares of forests were lost each year between 2000 and 2010. That's about the same size as the state of Louisiana or Alabama, every year.

DID YOU KNOW?

Deforestation makes up about 15 per cent of global greenhouse gas emissions.

Illegal logging

Some areas of forest are protected and no logging is allowed. In other areas, permits are needed so the number of trees cut down is controlled. Illegal logging is when trees are cut down without permission. It is a multi-million dollar industry and is thought to represent 15-30 per cent of all wood traded globally. It is threatening some of the world's most valuable forests such as the Amazon and the forests of the Russian Far East. An estimated 25 per cent of Russia's timber comes from illegal logging.

This map shows countries that have the highest rates of illegal logging. The US is one of the top consumers of wood from countries that are at high risk from illegal logging.

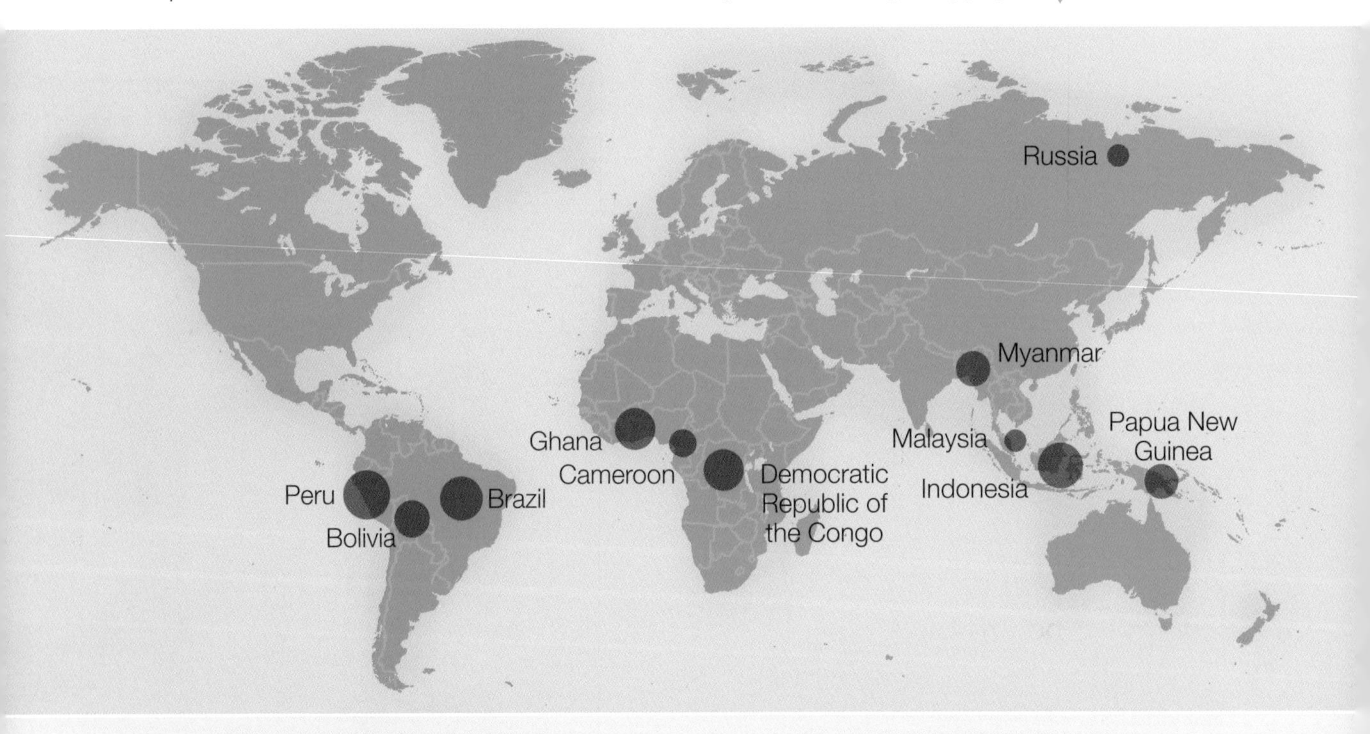

Fighting illegal loggers

Countries such as Brazil are fighting illegal logging by imposing high fines on illegal loggers. They are also employing forest rangers to use satellites to find areas of forest that are being cleared. But illegal loggers are becoming increasingly violent since the monetary rewards are so high. For example a cubic metre of rosewood can sell for £40,855 ($50,000) in China. Logging crews are often armed with guns, and rangers and local people have been killed for trying to stop them.

Using technology

Concerned groups such as Rainforest Foundation UK are using technology to fight illegal logging. They have introduced a system of smartphones that will allow local people to report any illegal logging or environmental crimes they see. In Brazil, Greenpeace have helped a local tribe to fight against illegal logging by supplying ten GPS tracking devices and a dozen camera traps. The tribespeople have placed the tracking devices on the logging trucks so they can see where they are going. The camera traps are usually used for filming wildlife but here they hope to catch evidence of lorries loaded with illegal logs.

Helping consumers

As a consumer, how do you know where the wood or paper you are buying comes from? This is why the Forest Stewardship Council (FSC) was set up over 20 years ago. The FSC is a global forest certification system. The FSC allows consumers to know that they are buying paper or wood products from forests that have been looked after to strict standards. Buyers just need to look for the "tick-tree" logo.

The FSC tick tree logo can only be used on certified products.

GOOD NEWS

Over 190 million hectares (470 million acres) of forest have been classed as being responsibly managed by the Forest Stewardship Council (FSC).

Conservation Finance

Very often the poorest countries have the most diverse environments that are in need of protection. The governments of these countries often have huge **debts** and struggle to find funds to look after their people, let alone their environments.

DID YOU KNOW?

80 per cent of deforestation in the next 15 years is likely to happen in just 11 places.

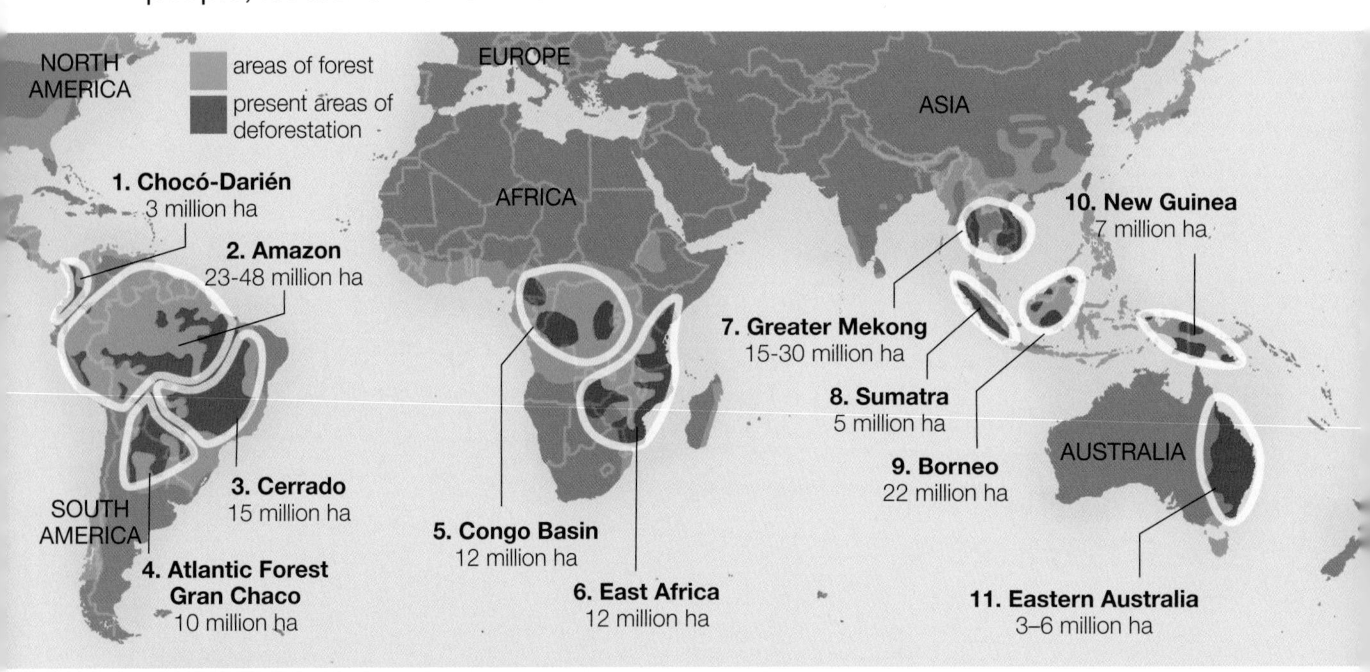

This map shows the 11 places most at risk of deforestation, and the figure beneath shows the estimated loss of hectares between 2010 and 2030.

Debt-for-nature swaps

Debt-for-nature swaps are when a developing country's debts are "bought" by other countries or organizations, such as World Wide Fund for Nature, on the agreement that the developing country then invests in protecting their environments.

In 2010, the US and Brazil agreed a debt-for-nature swap. Now Brazil, instead of paying the £17 million ($21) million back to the US, will use this to fund the conservation of its Atlantic coastal rainforest and the Cerrado and Caatinga ecosystems. These three areas are all threatened by deforestation. As well as conserving nature, the funds will be used to help boost the livelihoods of people who live in these areas.

Involving local communities

In many cases the poorest people are most affected by environmental damage such as deforestation or pollution. Yet it is these people who could help to protect their environment, if they had the funds. Some companies, such as the US-based not-for-profit Root Capital, offer local farmers training and short-term loans so that they can improve their farm's productivity and earn better prices for their crops. If local people are able to make a living from their environment by looking after it, then perhaps bribes and corruption won't seem so attractive.

GOOD NEWS

Protecting Brazil's Atlantic Forest could preserve hundreds of different species of trees. A recent study found that in just one hectare of this forest there were 450 different species of trees.

CASE STUDY:
Sustainable palm oil

Palm oil **plantations** have been blamed for the destruction of huge areas of tropical rainforests. Palm oil is the most widely used vegetable oil in the world. The oil palms, from which palm oil comes from, like to grow in the same climate as tropical rainforests. People can make money growing palm oil because it is in such demand and it has helped to lift people out of poverty. Unfortunately, in the past there have been incentives for growing palm oil that have resulted in forest destruction and the loss of wildlife. However, the good news is that it is possible to grow palm oil without causing such environmental problems.

Orangutan populations have been harmed by palm oil production. 

Good news

Forty per cent of global palm oil production is from members of the Roundtable on Sustainable Palm Oil (RSPO), which works with growers to promote better practices.

Serendipalm

Serendipalm is the world's first and largest **fair trade** and **organic** certified palm oil company. The company is made up of 670 farmer members and is showing that it is possible to grow palm oil without damaging the environment. It was set up in 2006 and now cultivates 4,000 acres of trees in Ghana, Africa.

Before Serendipalm was formed there were two types of palm oil farmers in Ghana. The first type of palm oil farmer could afford pesticides to grow more crops but their crops regularly suffered from chemical-related illness. The second type of palm oil farmer could not afford pesticides so couldn't grow as many crops and didn't earn as much money.

Now, Serendipalm farmers receive training on how to use organic farming techniques to grow more crops. They also get more money for their crops because organic palm oil is seen as a better product.

DID YOU KNOW?

Palm oil is used in many processed items including pizza dough, cookies, ice cream, chocolate, shampoo, soap and even lipstick.

How can we make a difference?

Protecting the environment is a massive global challenge and one that we can all play our part in. It might be that we can't personally save a rainforest but we can be responsible shoppers. We can look for the FSC logo (see page 35) on any paper or wood products that we buy. We can check whether the products we use contain palm oil and, if so, is it from a sustainable source? We can think about the environment before turning up the heating or getting into the car to drive instead of walking.

DID YOU KNOW?

Globally, at least 58 million disposable cups are used each year. Making this many cups each year emits the same amount of greenhouses gases as 500,000 cars.

Consumer choices all add up and can help make a difference. ▼

Reuse and recycle

We can take a reusable drinks bottle instead of buying another plastic bottle that may end up becoming part of a plasticky soup in the ocean. Taking our own bags to the shops will cut down on the number of plastic bags that we each use, and disposing of them responsibly will help to keep them out of the sea. Recycling other products we use, such as paper or aluminium cans, all helps to reduce the amount of rubbish we make.

Using alternative modes of transport needn't be boring.

THINK ABOUT IT

Anyone can make a difference. Kiara Nirghin is a 16-year-old student from South Africa. In 2016 she won a £38,000 ($50,000) science prize for her use of orange peel to create a very cheap absorbent material to reduce water loss in soil to help crops grow.

Human activity

Human activity is the cause of the majority of today's environmental issues. We know that burning fossil fuels and cutting down forests increases the level of greenhouse gases in Earth's atmosphere. We know about the effect of these greenhouse gases on the world's temperature. We understand that an increase in temperature will lead to rising sea levels and extremes of weather. Because we know these things we can take action to try to improve the situation.

DID YOU KNOW?

Apparently the ozone layer smells very faintly of the geranium plant.

Burning fossil fuels is the main human activity that affects the rate of climate change. ▲

Finding a new use for old fishing nets protects marine life and reduces ocean pollution.

Sea change

We are becoming increasingly aware of the important role our seas and oceans play in life on Earth. With this knowledge we have the power to do things differently and make a difference. People around the world have done just that. For example, unwanted fishing nets are sometimes just dumped at sea, but people in the Philippines have put these discarded fishing nets to good use. They have turned them into carpets which they can sell. This removes unwanted waste from the environment and helps the local people to earn money.

Sharing knowledge

If we share our knowledge then more people can be empowered to change their behaviour — even if it's just putting a jumper on instead of turning up the heating, or reading the label on products we buy. If we all do it, then many small actions add up to one big action.

GOOD NEWS

Young scientists are already inventing cheap, affordable ways to harness clean energy. Maanasa Mendu, a US student, was just 13 years old when she invented a way to convert sunlight, wind and rain into renewable energy. And her device only costs £4 ($5).

TIMELINE

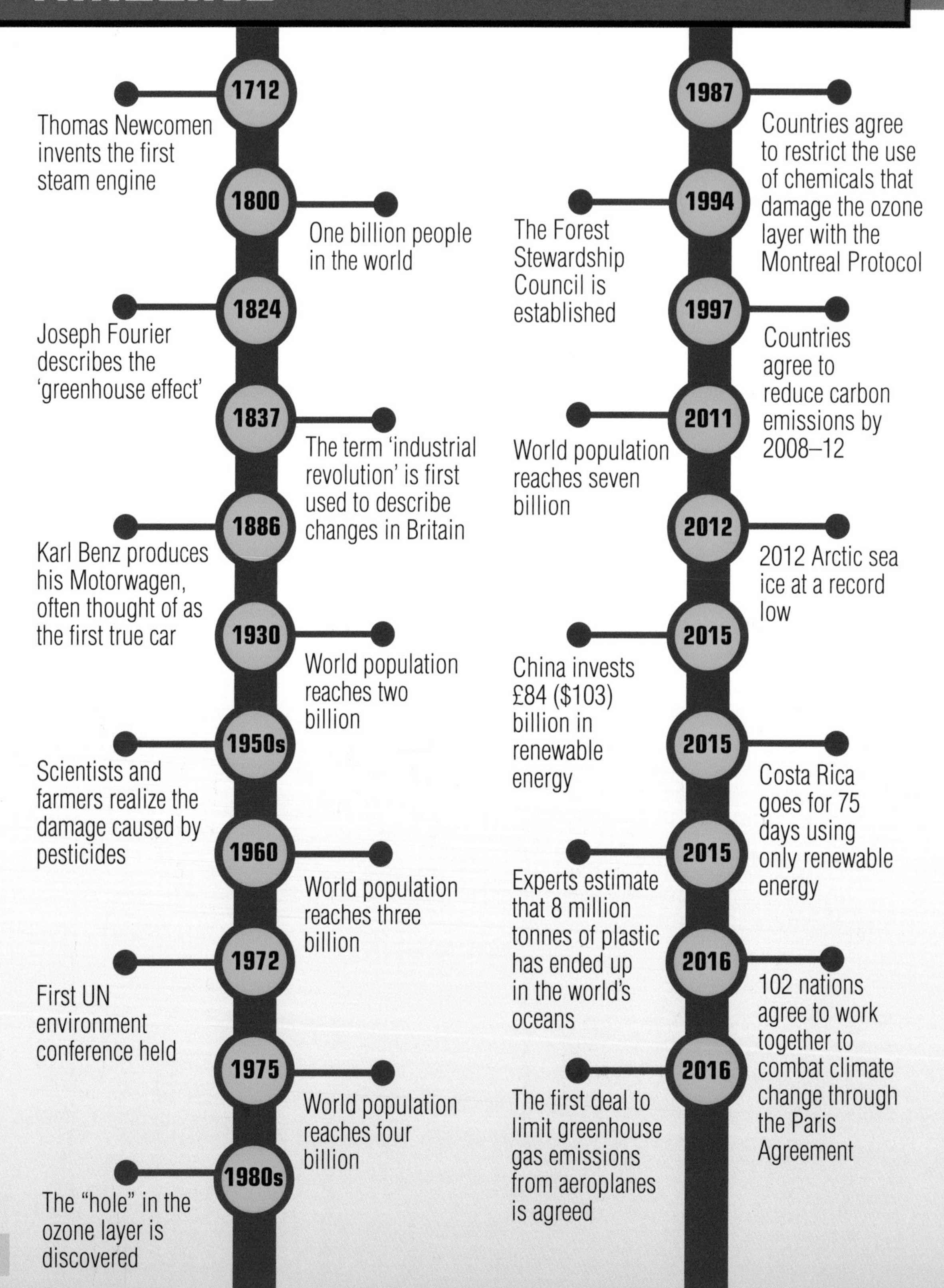

1712
Thomas Newcomen invents the first steam engine
1800
One billion people in the world
1824
Joseph Fourier describes the 'greenhouse effect'
1837
The term 'industrial revolution' is first used to describe changes in Britain
1886
Karl Benz produces his Motorwagen, often thought of as the first true car
1930
World population reaches two billion
1950s
Scientists and farmers realize the damage caused by pesticides
1960
World population reaches three billion
1972
First UN environment conference held
1975
World population reaches four billion
1980s
The "hole" in the ozone layer is discovered
1987
Countries agree to restrict the use of chemicals that damage the ozone layer with the Montreal Protocol
1994
The Forest Stewardship Council is established
1997
Countries agree to reduce carbon emissions by 2008–12
2011
World population reaches seven billion
2012
2012 Arctic sea ice at a record low
2015
China invests £84 ($103) billion in renewable energy
2015
Costa Rica goes for 75 days using only renewable energy
2015
Experts estimate that 8 million tonnes of plastic has ended up in the world's oceans
2016
102 nations agree to work together to combat climate change through the Paris Agreement
2016
The first deal to limit greenhouse gas emissions from aeroplanes is agreed

GLOSSARY

atmosphere the mixture of gases that surrounds the Earth

carbon chemical element, found in all living things, that is the basis for life

chemical pesticides substance made from chemicals used to kill pests such as insects

climate change a significant change in Earth's climate over a period of time

debt something that is owed

deforestation when trees and plants from a forest or woodland are cut down and not replaced

emissions substances released into the air

fair trade way of producing products where all people involved are rewarded fairly

Industrial Revolution a period from the middle 1700s to the 1800s of social and economic changes that took place during a transition from an agricultural and commercial society to an industrial society; the movement started in Great Britain and spread to Europe and the United States

lobby attempt to influence or sway a public official towards a desired action

organic using only natural products and no chemicals or pesticides

photosynthesis process by which plants make food using sunlight, carbon dioxide, and water

precipitation water that falls from clouds to the Earth's surface; precipitation can be rain, hail, sleet, or snow

renewable energy power from sources that will not be used up, such as wind, water, and the Sun

World War II a war in which the United States, France, Great Britain, the Soviet Union and other countries defeated Germany, Italy, and Japan; World War II lasted from 1939 to 1945.

tropics a warm region of Earth that is near the equator

turbine a machine with blades that can be turned by a moving fluid such as steam or water

ultraviolet an invisible form of light that can cause sunburn

FIND OUT MORE

When finding out more about environmental issues, remember to think about the reliability of the source — does it have an interest in persuading the reader to think in a particular way? Sometimes only certain information may be presented which means the reader doesn't gain the full picture of an issue.

National news websites, newspapers and journals such as *Nature*, are a good way of keeping up to date with the latest information about environmental issues.

Websites

www.greenpeace.org.uk
Greenpeace is an international organization that campaigns for environmental change.

oceanservice.noaa.gov/facts
National Ocean Service has a wealth of material about the ocean.

wwf.panda.org
The World Wide Fund for Nature is a conservation organization that aims to protect the natural environment. Its website has many interesting resources about nature and wildlife around the world and information on how you can involved.

Books

Are Humans Damaging the Atmosphere? (Earth Debates), Catherine Chambers (Raintree, 2015)

Critical Perspectives on Fossil Fuels vs. Renewable Energy (Analyzing the Issues), Anne Cunningham (Enslow Publishing, 2017)

How Effective Is Recycling? (Earth Debates), Catherine Chambers (Raintree, 2015)

How Harmful Are Fossil Fuels? (Earth Debates), Catherine Chambers (Raintree, 2015)

Saving the Environment (Charities in Action), Andrew Langley (Raintree, 2013)

INDEX